# From My Heart To Yours

## I Loved, I Lost, I Conquered

SHELIA TURNER

ISBN 978-1-64028-936-9 (Paperback)
ISBN 978-1-64028-937-6 (Digital)

Christian Faith Publishing, Inc.
296 Chestnut Street
Meadville, PA 16335
www.christianfaithpublishing.com

Printed in the United States of America

I dedicate this book to my children. I am not rich in dollars and cents, my wealth and riches come in the form of experience and wisdom, and I offer this to you. Hopefully, your mistakes and hardships will lessen and along with this I give my love, which I consider priceless.

As you travel down the highways and biways of life, check out your surroundings. There is one who sits high and looks low, he knows your troubles and he answers your prayers. His name is Jesus.

Let this book be like food to your soul.

Read it. Digest it. Live it.

# Introduction

This book is about my love, my faith, and how it changed my life. My hope is that it will lift your spirit, strengthen your faith, and bring joy into your life.

All power is in God's hands and in order to grow spiritually and have inner peace we must trust in his holy word.

I CAN DO ALL THINGS THROUGH
CHRIST WHICH STRENGTHENS ME.

—Philippians 4:13

# Acknowledgments

God, thank you for building a fence around me and showing me the true meaning of love. Thank you for your grace and mercy and thank you for taking me on a journey to a better understanding.

Traune and Tawanna, thank you for loving me and showing me your strengths. Thank you for my adorable grandchildren.

Brothers Kent and Robert, I miss you so much.

Cousin Elaine, there will never be a friendship that I treasure more than the one we had.

Dad, you taught me so much, being your caregiver gave me a whole new insight on life, people, and family.

Mom, you started me going to church. At one time I strayed, but your teachings lead me back.

My siblings, we laughed, we played, and at times we fought, but the bond we had always overpowered any disagreement, because of our love.

THE LORD IS MY SHEPHERD; I SHALL NOT
WANT. HE MAKETH ME LIE DOWN IN
GREEN PASTURES; HE LEADS ME BESIDE

THE STILL WATERS, HE RESTORES MY
SOUL; HE LEADS ME IN THE PATH OF
RIGHTEOUSNESS FOR HIS NAME SAKE. YEA
THOUGH I WALK THROUGH THE VALLEY OF
THE SHADOW OF DEATH, I WILL FEAR NO
EVIL; FOR YOU ARE WITH ME; YOUR ROD
AND YOUR STAFF, THEY COMFORT ME.

YOU PREPARED A TABLE BEFORE ME IN THE
PRESENCE OF MY ENEMIES; YOU ANOINT MY
HEAD WITH OIL; MY CUP RUNS OVER, SURELY
GOODNESS AND MERCY SHALL FOLLOW ME
ALL THE DAYS OF MY LIFE; AND I WILL DWELL
IN THE HOUSE OF THE LORD FOREVER.

— Psalms 23

# Family

My mom passed away in 1963. She was a loving mother, the organist for the church. She devoted her time making sure we were raised properly. After my mom's death, my dad assigned us permanent duties. We worked together to make things work.

Dad was a strict disciplinarian, a good provider. He taught us the importance of giving, especially to those less fortunate than ourselves.

As a teenager, I didn't make his job raising me very easy, but when I became a parent, I understood his pain and concern. I realized what parenting was all about.

As siblings we laughed, we played, and we fought. The bond between us was strong, even through our disagreements.

Our love for each other outweighed everything.

# Journey

In 1968, I left home seeking employment in Washington, DC. After a couple of months I was employed with the government. I enjoyed the single life, had my own apartment, doing my own thing. After a while, I was tired of the single life. I met my husband. He was living in Delaware, and we traveled back and forth for a while. We married March 30, 1974, and of that union, we have two children.

After several years in the Maryland/ DC area. We decided we would raise our children in a more quiet and stable environment, so we moved to Virginia. We were both employed and later decided to attend college. After completing our studies, we were planning to purchase our first house and make Richmond, Virginia, our home, a new house, a new location, new surroundings, but unfortunately, without the man I married and the father of my children.

On April 8, 1984, paramedics informed me my husband was killed in an auto accident. This left a big void in my life. I never doubted I couldn't make it. I just knew it wouldn't be easy. At this time, I was undecided what my next move would be. I asked for extended leave from my job.

I decided to move home with Dad for a while. Being home gave me a clearer picture of what I needed to do. I decided to move to Hampton, Virginia. School was about to start, and I need to get things in order. August 1984 we moved into our new house. We were well on our way.

When I felt my children were well adjusted, I decided to pursue my dream and open my own salon. In 1986, I became a license cosmetologist. I was getting my life back on track when I discovered a lump in my breast. I scheduled an appointment to see a doctor, and he scheduled me for a biopsy. My fear was confirmed. When you hear the word *cancer*, you immediately think *death*, and being a single parent made it even more devastating. I didn't know how to tell my children who were eight and nine years old at the time that they were going to lose their mom as well. I decided not to tell them. They never knew the full extent of my illness. I decided to focus on surviving. Through prayer and perseverance, I am able to tell my story.

> For God has not given us the spirit of fear, but
> of power, and of love and a sound mind.
>
> —II Timothy 1:7

# Surgery

September 1986, I entered the hospital to undergo surgery. A mastectomy which was about to be life-changing for me. My will to live overpowered the fear I had of the disfigurement of any change I was about to endure. I looked into the eyes of my fatherless children, and nothing else mattered. I asked God to keep me here so I might see my children grow and be able to care for themselves.

I kept the faith and God delivered.

I hope someday there will be a cure for cancer. Only those who have experience this disease can truly relate. This disease robs you of your immune system, it kills good cells while destroying the bad ones, it can leave you disfigured, and after you go through so much, you are faced with high medical bills and insurance companies that will drop you or charge such a high deductible that you cannot afford insurance.

The sisterhood of breast cancer survivors should always be strong, and we must stand united to support the cause. I wear my pink with pride and dignity knowing the challenges cancer victims face.

# Healing

After surgery, I returned home, all bandaged, not knowing the full extent of my recovery. A friend drove me home from the hospital. We sat overlooking a large body of water, and suddenly, a calming feeling came over me. I felt this inner peace. Everything appeared brighter. The trees, the water, and all my surroundings. I felt everything was going to be okay.

The day of therapy I walked into the clinic, and there were people hooked up to a machine with IVs in their arms, with a solution slowly dripping in their veins. Most had lost their hair. Again I was in tears. I thought to myself, I don't belong here, but of course, cancer does not strike any particular race, age, or gender.

My therapy lasted nine months. I experienced hair loss, fatigue, nausea, and many other symptoms. There were times after treatments I was so weak, I found myself crawling in my house to get where I needed to go.

The battle was long and difficult. My faith kept me strong and make me well. I am thankful for a second chance.

# Getting Established

While getting established as a hairstylist, trying to build my clientele, raising two children was not easy. I mustered the strength to go to work while taking chemotherapy. In 1988, I opened my own salon, where I employed, nail technicians hairstylists, barbers, and wax technicians, but I wanted to give back in some way.

I became a volunteer for the Look Good, Feel Better Program for the American Cancer Society and eventually opened an area in my salon for cancer survivors to provide them with scarves, turbans, wigs, and hairpieces that would make them feel better about their appearance while going through chemotherapy.

I recalled being in a class, assisting ladies with their makeup and showing them how to wear their head wraps. There was one lady who came in with a sad face. Her husband dropped her off. When he returned and saw her all made up and smiling, he thanked us over and over again. He said he had not seen her smile in a while.

Life is making sure it's meaningful and making sure you are a service to others.

As each one has received a gift, let
him minister one to another.

—1 Peter 4:10

# *Certificate of Service*

Presented to:

In appreciation of *four years* of volunteer
service to the program. (date)

Recognizing your continuing dedication to helping women
overcome the appearance-related side effects of cancer.

# Testimony

God brought me through the turbulence of life. He sheltered me from all harm and danger. I am thankful for the gift of love and many prayers answered, especially during my battle with cancer.

He gave me a second chance.

Again I rise!

# Second Chance

I want to take this opportunity to let all cancer survivors know that it is within itself a blessing to have survived such an awful disease. One is not defined by the scars and/or disfigurement of one's body. It's always been beauty of the heart. Most people I've talked with that have survived cancer always say, and I quote, "I no longer take life for granted."

Today I have a different outlook on life. I clearly see the seriousness of God's need for us to love one another. I realize in spite of my insecurities at the time, I am the same person on the inside.

We are not defined by shapely bodies, clear complexions, straight hair—the things we deem as beauty. God sees our soul. If we are not able to understand the completeness of God's provision, we will not be able to be at peace with what we have and who we are.

I am so thankful when I entered the doctor's office in August 1986 that I was not told I only had a week or few months to live. God extended the gift of life to me. He guided me through a journey of understanding. He taught me patience, which I so badly needed. He let me see firsthand how riches and wealth come in many forms. God measures wealth by the quality of our lives and our generous distribution of wealth to bless others.

If we have been blessed with riches, we must be rich in deeds. God wants us to be generous meeting other's needs. He has given me peace of mind. I pray for peace of mind for all mankind.

Peace on Earth, Good Will Toward Man

God help mankind
To find a peace that will be right and just,
A peace of all nations where man can place their faith and trust.
God help men
To see the foolish course they travel
And pursue and that no place on earth
can be without the aid of you.
God open wide the eyes of men
To understand and see,
Peace must be based on faith and trust to make all nations free.

# *Losses*

September 2005, my cousin Elaine passed away from breast cancer. Elaine was my partner in crime and my best friend. I shared so much with her. I miss our conversations, our lunch and dinner dates and our frequent out of town trips. Elaine's beautiful and bubbly personality would always bring so much joy to those around her.

July 2008, my youngest brother Kent passed away of a heart attack, and one week later, my oldest brother Robert passed away of lung cancer.

My fondest memory of Kent was at my sixtieth birthday party. He had so much fun. He always wore a smile, and Robert was always the first to call me on holidays.

*As we journey through life, we need to look around, touch someone, help the needy, take time to comfort the disabled and weary, reach out to the addict and alcoholic, and embrace the elderly, which we so often forget.*

Dorothy Pope
My mom

Benjamin Pope
Dad

Lawrence Turner
Husband
Deceased

Kent
Deceased Brother

Elaine (Cousin)
Deceased

Lawrence & Mildred Turner
Deceased
Father and Mother-In-Law

Robert Hill
Deceased
Brother

# Taking Nothing for Granted

I retired from my business and later worked a part-time job at a library. It gave me some insight on life. It has given me an appreciation of just how blessed I am.

I see the homeless trying to keep cool on not muggy days and trying to keep warm on cool breezy days.

I couldn't help but wonder what must be going through their minds. I have a warm/cool place to go to every day. I have a family to spend my holidays with.

We take so much for granted. We always expect more, when we fail to realize we have plenty. Let us not forget the less fortunate.

# Taking Care of Dad

In 2013, I moved in with Dad to care for him. He was a diabetic and was experiencing memory loss and kidney failure. As his POA, I had to sign all of his papers and make all medical decisions. He had to get his toes amputated and later his leg. Signing those papers was one of the hardest things I had to do. He required twenty-four-hour care. I was able to select two wonderful caregivers, which covered sixteen hours a day, and the other eight hours I care for my dad. It was a very exhausting task. Knowing my dad who was so independent and then seeing him having to depend on someone was so hard.

Dad was placed in hospice, and of course, his care became more intense. I thank God for giving me the strength to care for him.

When you are left without parents, it can be a lonely place. I have peace of mind knowing I was there for my dad, and I did all I could to care for him. I know he is in a better place.

When siblings are left without parents, it's a loss like no other.

There should never be a price tag on family values. Many families have been destroyed because of greed or just resentment of one sibling having authority over another. The things we possess in life, through whatever means is done through the love and grace of God.

Our parents gave us each other, life is precious, tomorrow is not promised, when the day is done, all we have is each other.

# Serenity Prayer

. . . . . . . . . . . . . . . .

God, grant me the serenity to except the things I cannot change, the courage to change the things I can, and the wisdom to know the difference.

# Special Prayer

. . . . . . . . . . . . . . . .

Father, I come before you wanting to know more about you, wanting to walk in you likeness. Cleanse my heart and renew in me a right spirit. Without you, I am nothing.

Help me to be a forgiving person. Give me strength to endure the obstacles that come my way.

Let the joy of your word fill my heart with peace and happiness and I forever rest in the arms of righteousness.

# On the Wings of Prayer

Just close your eyes
and open your heart
And feel your worries
and cares depart,
Just yield yourself
to the Father above let
Him hold you secure in His love.

# Words of Encouragement

## Problems

. . . . . . . . . .

If we put our problems in God's hands
There is nothing we need understand—
It is enough to just believe that what we need we will receive.
Life is a mixture of sunshine and rain,
Teardrops and laughter, pleasure and pain—
We can't have all bright days, but it's certainly true,
There was never a cloud the sun didn't shine through!
Everything is by comparison, both the bitter and the sweet,
And it takes a bit of both of them to make our lives complete.
(Helen Steiner Rice)

## Sickness

. . . . . . . . . .

Sometimes the things that seem the worst turn out to be the best—so think of this as just a time to get a little rest—and while you cannot understand why things happen as they do—the one who hangs the rainbow out has his own plans for you—and may it comfort you to know that you are in his care and you are all apart of God and God is *everywhere*!

## Stressed

· · · · · · · · · ·

This Too, Will Pass Away

If I can endure for this minute, whatever is happening to me, no matter how heavy my heart is, or how dark the moment may be. If I can remain calm and quiet with all my world crashing about me, when everyone else seems to doubt me. If I can keep on believing what I know in my heart to be true, that darkness will fade with the morning and that will pass away too, then nothing in life can defeat me, for as long as this knowledge remains, I can suffer whatever is happening, for I know God will break all the chains that are binding me tight in the darkness and trying to fill me with fear. For there is no night without dawning and I know my morning is near.

## Teachings of Wisdom, Understanding, and Knowledge

· · · · · · · · · · · · · · · · · · · · · · · · · · · · · ·

God's Knowledge
Proverbs 2:1

My son if thy will receive my words, and hide my commandments with thee,

So that thine decline thy ear unto wisdom, and apply thy heart unto understanding;

Yea, if thy cry after knowledge, and lifted up thine heart to understanding;

If thou see her as silver, and search for her as hid treasure;

Then shall thou understand the fear of the Lord, and find the knowledge of God.

Obedience and behavior
Proverbs 13:1–9

A wise man hearth his father's instructions, but a scorner hearth not rebuke

A man shall eat good by the fruit of his mouth, but the soul of the transgressors shall eat violence

He that keepest in mouth, keepest his life, he that open wide his lips shall have destruction

The soul of the sluggish disireth, and hath nothing, but the soul of the diligent shall be made Fat

A righteous man hath lying, but a wick man is loathsome, and cometh to shame

Righteousness keep him that is upright in the way; but wickedness over throw the sinner

There is that make himself rich, yet hath nothing, there is that make himself poor, yet has great riches

The ransom of a man's life are his riches, but the poor hear not rebuke.

The light of the righteous rejoice; but the lamp of the wicked shall be put out

Only the pride cometh contention, but with the well advised is wisdom

Wealth gotten by vanity shall be dismissed, but he that gather labor shall increase

Hope deferred make the heart sick; but then the desire cometh, it is the tree of life

Whoso despise the word shall be destroyed, but he that fear the commandment shall be rewarded

The law of the wise is the fountain of life, to depart from the snares of death

Good understanding give favor; but the ways of transgressor is hard

Every prudent man deals with knowledge; but a fool lay open his folly

A wicked messenger fall into mischief; but a faith ambassador is health

Poverty and shame shall be to him that refuse instruction, but the regarded reproof shall be honored.

The desired accomplished is sweet to the soul, but it is an abomination to fools to depart from evil.

In God we trust
Proverbs 3:1–6

My son, forget not my law, but let thine heart keep my commandments;

For length of days and long life and peace shall they add to thee;

Let not mercy and truth forsake thee; bind them about the neck, write them upon the table of thine heart

So shall thine find favor and good understanding in the sight of God and man

Trust in the Lord with all thine heart and lean not to thy own understanding

In all thy ways I knowledge him and he will direct your path.

# Reflections

## Rest
• • • • • •

When I'm troubled and confused, I need spiritual rest.
This gives me a chance to listen and reflect.
Be still, learn to rest in Him to do as the spirit directs.

—Psalms 46:10

## Salvation
• • • • • • • • • • •

You paid the price!

And this is the testimony that God has given us,
eternal life, and this life is in His son.

—1 John 5:11

# *Life*
......

Life's journey teaches us there will be problems, sickness, and disappointments.

We can rise against adversity. God serves many purposes; when you are sick, he is your healer (Psalms 103). When you can't meet you obligations, he is your deliver (Psalms 7:05). And when you are going through a difficult time, he is your guiding light (Isaiah W:20)

Call on Him.

# Words of Wisdom

# Tawanna

You were and still are my precious, pretty baby girl. I am so proud of you. You have proven to be a terrific mom and a woman of great strength. I have always admired that in you. Like your mom, you do not like your space invaded, but sometimes, it's good to let people in, especially those who love you.

You are deserving of all the great things God has for you; you must love yourself enough to feel worthy of receiving them.

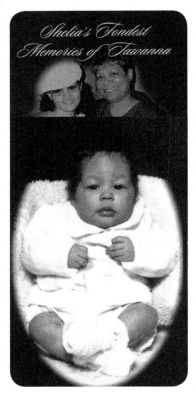

Shelia's Fondest Memories of Tawanna

## Fondest Memory

I received a card from you expressing your love and appreciation for the many things I've gone through as your mom and how you can now understand where I was coming from at the time. You were a handful. It was worth every minute I spent being a strong disciplinarian. Just look at you now. You are a beautiful person, a wonderful daughter, a good cook, a terrific mom, one beautiful person inside and out. Thank you.

# Traune

· · · · · · · · ·

You are my firstborn. I am so proud of you. Your dad was so pleased to have a son to carry on the Turner name.

You have always been a mama's boy. There is nothing wrong with that. The man who loves and respects his mom will love and respect his wife. Any woman would be so lucky.

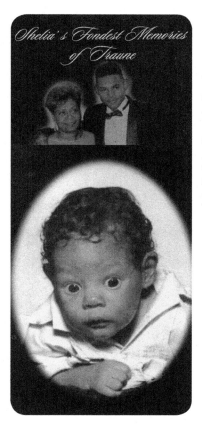

## Fondest Memory

· · · · · · · · · · · · · · · · · · ·

One mother's day, you gave me a CD entitled *Mama* by Boys II Men. You sang that song to me, and you expressed to me that my love for you was like food to your soul. Your singing hurt my ears but warmed my heart.

Thank you.

## *Then there were six:*

· · · · · · · · · · · · · · · · · · · · · ·

—Tiaura—

—Allen—

—Isaiah—

—Messiah—

—Dream—

—Tristian—

## Tiaura

· · · · · · · ·

The beauty that is shown on the outside must always shine on the inside. This is where one's true beauty is.

I believe in you. Use the many gifts God has given you. Remember, you would tell me you couldn't do certain things, and I would tell you, if you think you can't, you never will.

Not everything that is faced in life can be changed but, nothing can be changed until it is faced.

## Allen "Deuce"

· · · · · · · · · · · · · · · · ·

You are a handsome young man. You will one day break many hearts (smile), but remember, a real man respects his lady, and if he gives respect not just to his lady, but all ladies, he will get respect.

I hope you will continue to do what makes you happy, whether it's playing basketball or singing. Just believe I will always be your loudest cheerleader. I believe in you.

## Isaiah

. . . . . . . .

We call you the professor because you are so knowledgeable. You take the most complicated things and fix them.

I see great things happening for your future. Never give up on your dreams. I will be cheering you on.

# Messiah

· · · · · · · · · ·

You are my little mini me. You are very smart, and I see a bright future for you. Your ability to win hearts as you do

Show me you will achieve great things.

You are a people person, very confident, and fearless. Keep smiling and being compassionate toward others, and God will take you to great heights.

## *Dream*

· · · · · · · · ·

You have a personality like no other, and your beautiful smile, and your hugs and kisses always win me over.

Never forget our favorite song. Truly you are my sunshine.

## *Tristian*

· · · · · · · · · ·

It was such a joy for us the day you were born. You are a happy little boy; your bubbly personality keeps me smiling.

Hugs and kisses to you my little man.

## Life's Certainties

There is one thing in life that is certain, and that is we will someday depart from this earth. What we do between birth and death is our choice.

"We are the masters of our fate; we are the captains of our souls" (William Ernest Henley)

## I Loved

I married a wonderful man. Of that union, we have two wonderful children, and because of that union, I now have six grandchildren. We shared his love and will forever share his memory.

## I Lost

The loss of my mom, my husband, my brothers, my cousin, and my dad left a big void. I thank God for them, for it is better to have loved and lost than never to have loved at all.

## I Conquered

God brought me through it all. He opened my eyes that I might see clearly my surroundings—the good, the bad, the ugly. I know who I am and whose I am. He built a fence around me and protected me from all harm and danger. He allowed me the time I asked for and that was to see my children grow up to be able to care for themselves. Not only am I able to see my children grow but also able to enjoy my grandchildren as well.

Tiaura, Allen, Isaiah, Messiah, Dream, and Tristian.

## /Mimi's Babies/

I hope after reading this book you have been inspired in some way to help you face life's challenges with a positive attitude, and believing God is in control.

We may never understand why things happen as they do, but knowing God won't take you on a journey to leave you to fight your battles alone should be refreshing and rewarding.

GOD BLESS YOU

"JESUS THE LIGHT OF THE WORLD!!!

# About the Author

Shelia L. Turner, born November 29,1947 to Benjamin and Dorothy Pope, there were six siblings. Two deceased.

I attended Hayden High School and later moved to Washington DC where I worked for the government. I married Lawrence Turner March 1974 and of that union we have two children, Traune and Tawanna, and today we have six grandchildren who call me MiMi.

I attend New Grafton Baptist Church in Newport News, VA.

I am involved in two ministries, The Beautification Ministry and The Community Links Ministry.

My favorite scripture is Philippians 4:13, "I can do all things through Christ with strengthens me". My favorite time of the year is Spring, I love seeing God's work in progress, watching the flowers and trees with their beautiful colors bloom.

My favorite two gospels songs are "I won't complain" and "God keep Me Day By Day".

I became a hairstylist in 1986 and opened my own salon in 1988 and retired in 2005.

I am a cancer survivor.

There are a few things in life I live by and they are: Don't be afraid to pursue your dreams, if you think you can you will, and small minds produce small results.

My most significant moments were when my two children were born and then my grandchildren, and certainly the day I was told my cancer was in remission.

I was inspired to write this book as a testimony to how God has given me a "second chance". I dedicate this book to my children so that they can reflect on the life I've lived and the love and blessings I've recieved and hope they will understand how powerful God is and how grateful I am to be given this time on earth to enjoy their presence, and to the readers, I hope in some way I have inspired you.

God Bless

CPSIA information can be obtained
at www.ICGtesting.com
Printed in the USA
LVOW06s2309230817
546082LV00036B/877/P

9 781640 289369